W9-AOU-136

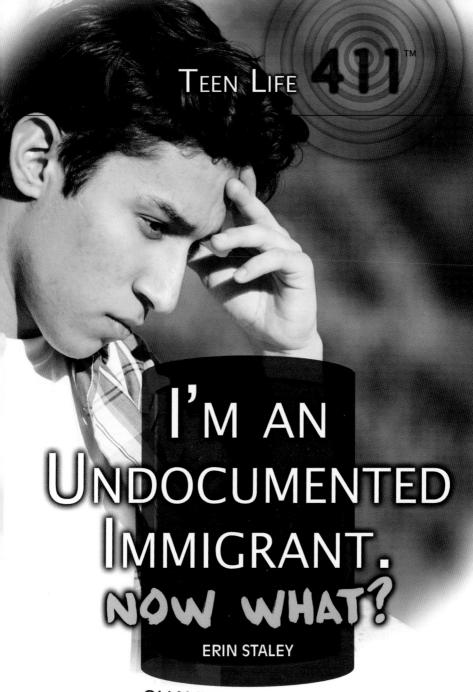

I'M AN UNDOCUMENTED IMMIGRANT.
NOW WHAT?

ERIN STALEY

ROSEN
PUBLISHING®

New York

Published in 2017 by The Rosen Publishing Group, Inc.
29 East 21st Street, New York, NY 10010

Copyright © 2017 by The Rosen Publishing Group, Inc.

First Edition

Library of Congress Cataloging-in-Publication Data

Names: Staley, Erin.
Title: I'm an undocumented immigrant. Now what? / Erin Staley.
Description: First edition. | New York : Rosen Publishing, 2017. | Series: Teen life 411 | Includes bibliographical references and index. |
Identifiers: LCCN 2016028548 | ISBN 9781508171935 (library bound)
Subjects: LCSH: Illegal aliens—United States—Juvenile literature. | Immigrant youth—United States—Juvenile literature. | United States—Emigration and immigration—Juvenile literature.
Classification: LCC JV6483 .S65 2017 | DDC 305.235086/912—dc23
LC record available at https://lccn.loc.gov/2016028548

Manufactured in Malaysia

Contents

According to the Pew Research Center, there were 11.3 million unauthorized immigrants in the United States in 2014. They came in search of the "American Dream," but live in fear of being discovered and deported because of their illegal status. An "undocumented immigrant" is one who is in a country without government permission. This person may have come to the country on a non immigrant visa and overstayed the expiration date. Or this person may have entered without inspection (EWI). This means that no interaction took place between that individual and a US Border official. Then there are those who are in the process of gaining permanent residence, but have yet to acquire their legal documentation.

Undocumented immigrants are commonly referred to as "undocumented Americans." Children, tweens, and teenagers without legal status are often called "undocumented youth" or "DREAMers." If they were foreign-born but live in the United States with a parent and a younger US-born sibling, they are considered to be a part of the 1.5 Generation. Terms that are insensitive and ought to be avoided include "anchor baby," "unauthorized," and "illegal aliens."

Mary Tamer recognizes the undocumented youth population in "The Education of Immigrant Children" (2014):

Undocumented status affects more than 1 million children today, which is about one-third of all immigrant youth. Another 4.5 million US-born youth have an undocumented parent. Children face barriers because of their parents' undocumented status, often related to poverty, fears of deportation, and more, while undocumented youth themselves face increasing barriers to social mobility as they enter adolescence and hope to obtain driver's licenses, afterschool work, and financial aid for college. Even when children themselves are unaware of their family members' legal status, being undocumented or the child of an undocumented parent negatively impacts a child's development.

Immigrants from all over the world come to the United States. Some with adventurous spirits, seeking opportunity. Others who are fleeing political upheavel, religious oppression, or environmental disasters.

Being an undocumented American can be very lonely. You live in the shadows of being identified and deported, separated from everyone you love and everything you know. This fear could prevent you from getting involved and connecting with others. You may avoid playing sports, joining the debate team, going to the big dance, or meeting up with friends at a popular hangout. Mistrust, stress, anxiety, depression, and anger could result, further complicating your mental and physical well-being. But you are not alone. There is help within your community and on a national scale.

Advocacy groups, faith-based programs, educational institutes, and nonprofit organizations work to support, advise, and finance undocumented immigrants in their efforts to pursue an education, understand their rights, get a job, and seek legal status. Government policies and programs are in place to help you stay in the country, provided qualifications are met and maintained. And immigration attorneys are available to help navigate the nation's complicated and lengthy immigration process. Many of these resources are detailed in this book, helping you—or those you know—have the peace of mind and the knowledge needed to create your American Dream.

CHAPTER 1

Undocumented immigrants are those who have either entered or remained in the United States without legal documentation. Some are aware of their illegal status, and others are not. The American Psychological Association (APA) reports that there are 4.5 million US citizen children with unauthorized parents. Then there are another 1.5 million who are undocumented youths. No matter their circumstances, these youngsters live in fear. They live in the shadows, afraid of being discovered by government officials who could forcibly take them from loved ones, only to be dropped into the child welfare system, sent to detention centers, and deported to their country of origin. These fears bring on feelings of isolation, mistrust, stress, anxiety, depression, and anger.

GROWING UP AS "UNDOCUMENTED AMERICANS"

The APA's video, *Undocumented Americans*, features the real-life stories of three undocumented youths: Jong-Min, Silvia, and Pedro.

WHO ARE UNDOCUMENTED IMMIGRANTS?

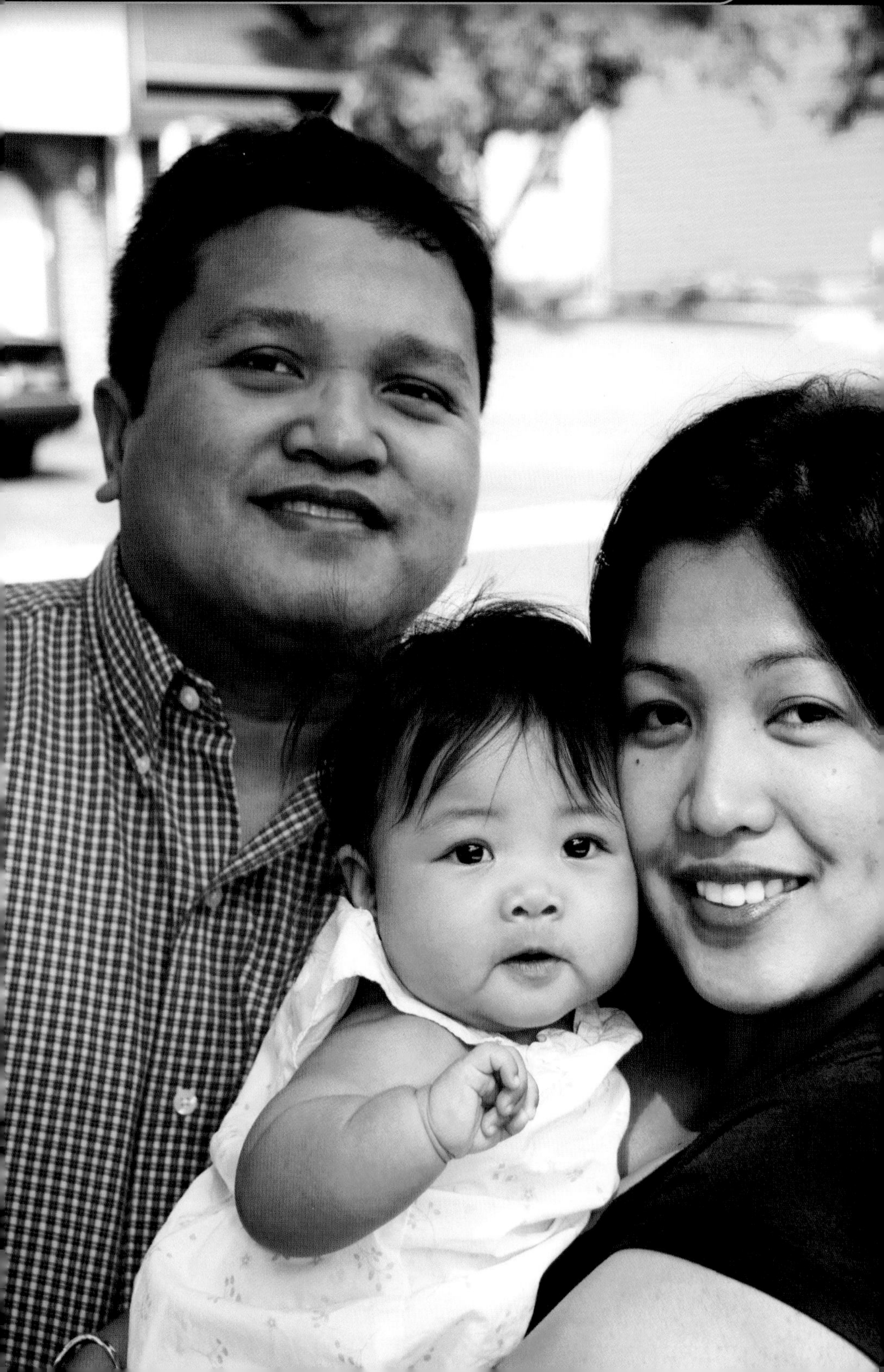

Each came to the United States at a young age, and has unique stories to share.

"I always thought I was legal in a sense," says Korean-born Jong-Min, recalling how shocked he was to learn of his illegal status. He had felt "American in every sort of way." His parents warned him not to reveal the family's status. They were afraid of deportation. Jong-Min soon recognized the limitations he faced. He wasn't able to do what his peers did. "Being undocumented is like living in this invisible prison," he says. "I'm American, and this is my home. This is my country."

Pedro came to the United States as a four-year-old. He was heartbroken when he learned of his family's illegal status. "I had to learn to be below the radar in everything I did, staying out of trouble, doing well in school," he says. "And I was never outside of my home unless I had a good reason for it." Pedro credits his siblings for being good role models. He worked hard in school, and was later accepted to Cornell University. Pedro even received scholarships. However, the threat of deportation lingered. In 2008, while traveling from Chicago to Cornell University, his bus was stopped by a Border Patrol agent. The agent questioned each passenger. Pedro admitted that he wasn't a US citizen. The college student was arrested. He was fingerprinted, made

Many immigrants arrive in the United States at a time in their lives when they are considering starting a family. This can lead to separation—and heartache—if proper documentation is not attained.

to strip and wear an orange jumpsuit, and held in a federal marshals prison in New York. "There was no one there that I felt was on my side. It was me versus everything," he says. "I was fighting for my freedom to be in this country." Pedro was released after twenty-four hours.

Silvia, a first-generation student, had high hopes of going to college. She just didn't have the money to pay for it. She applied for and was awarded a full scholarship to Arizona State University. But Arizona voters passed legislation that cut Silvia's financial aid and scholarship. She was also

Supporters of President Obama's DAPA and DACA policies on immigration and deportation are pictured here at the Supreme Court in Washington, DC, on April 18, 2016.

WAVES OF IMMIGRATION IN THE UNITED STATES

The United States has always been a land of immigrants. They come from around the world to live the American Dream—often without documentation to prove their identity and country of origin. The United States has experienced four waves of immigration. The first was from 1600 to 1820. Immigrants fled religious persecution in England, a poor economy in Germany, and religious repression in Scandinavian countries. Immigrants from the Netherlands came in search of trade, and immigrants from Africa were forced into the US slave trade.

The next wave came between 1820 and 1880. Irish immigrants escaped famine, and Chinese immigrants left bleak economic opportunities. By 1850, 2.2 million immigrants had already arrived, as noted in 2016 by the Migration Policy Institute (MPI). Russian immigrants also come in the late 1800s and early 1900s, escaping poverty and religious persecution. The third wave came sixty years later with Europeans, Mexicans, Japanese, Armenians, and Cubans fleeing war, poverty, and agricultural hardships. They pursued employment, refuge, and education. The fourth came in the 1960s. Immigration rapidly increased as Asian and Latin American immigrants left behind natural disasters, economic struggles, corrupt governments, and civil wars. MPI notes, "Since 1970, the number of US immigrants more than quadrupled, rising from 9.6 million in 1970 to 42.4 million in 2014."

Today, it's not as easy to migrate to the United States as it once was. Immigration laws are more strictly enforced, and borders are tightly controlled. If foreign-born people want to legally live and work in the United States, they must go thorough a lengthy and expensive application process for legal documentation. If requirements are not met in full, undocumented immigrants are required by law to return to their country of origin.

reclassified as an out-of-state student. This meant that
she had to pay nearly four times as much as what in-
state students had to pay. "It was really depressing to
know that the community there didn't want me," she
says. "But I wanted to be there and help the community
so much." Silvia put herself through school and eventually graduated. Yet, she couldn't get a job because she
didn't have proper documentation. Silvia forged ahead
and was accepted into graduate school at Harvard
University. Not eligible for financial aid, she started a
fund-raising campaign to cover her tuition. Silvia graduated from Harvard and went on to pursue her doctorate
degree at UCLA. However, the threat of deportation still
existed for Silvia's family. "I was in my finals at Harvard,
and my sister's high school was calling Immigration on
my mom in Texas," she says. Silvia flew out the next day.
Immigration had let her mother go, but she was afraid
that they'd come looking for her at her home. In the
process of fleeing, Silvia's mother had a seizure. She was
treated at a hospital but was later deported.

WHY DO IMMIGRANTS COME TO THE UNITED STATES?

There are many reasons why undocumented immigrants
come to the United States. They may be refugees, escaping corrupt and unfair governments. They may have
been denied rights and freedoms because of their race,
beliefs, customs, and political views. They hope for

Refugees flee war in Syria, arriving on the shores of Turkey in 2015. They had very little, and they started a new life in a new land.

equality and opportunity in a new land. Some undocumented immigrants are escaping natural disasters, such as hurricanes, droughts, and earthquakes. Their homes have been demolished, and a fresh start can save them from disease and starvation. Some immigrants may want to reunite with a spouse, parent, or child already living in the United States. Others may be in search of a better life for their children. This may include everything from getting a better education to living a life without the violence and crime that exists in their country of origin. Finally, some immigrants may find that the United States has an abundance of employment opportunities for those who work hard.

WHAT IS LEGAL DOCUMENTATION?

"If given a choice, opinion surveys of undocumented immigrants indicate that 98 percent would prefer to live and work legally in the United States and would do so if they could," reported the American Immigration Council in 2013. In order to do this, they would need legal documentation.

The highest form of legal status is citizenship. This allows one the permanent right to live and work in the United States. One has to either be born in the United States, or have parent that is a US citizen. These individuals are given a state-issued US birth certificate as legal documentation. It acts as one's primary proof of citizenship. Citizens cannot be deported. They have the right to vote, and they can petition for foreign-born family members to join them in the United States. Citizenship can also be extended to immigrants who meet specific qualifications. It is a very lengthy process, and one with many complicated steps.

Those who want to legally immigrate to the United States permanently need to be petitioned, or be sponsored by a spouse, relative, or employer. They can also be a refugee seeking asylum or a winner of the Diversity Visa Lottery (a program that distributes a limited number of visas each year). If immigrants meet the eligibility requirements, they are given a Legal Permanent Resident (LPR) card. This is commonly referred to as a "green card." Green cards act as proof that an immigrant has the right to live and work in the United States. Those

with an LPR can access government benefits, receive
federal student financial aid, enlist in the US military,
and travel internationally without asking for permission. They can even sponsor a spouse and children to
receive their own green cards. Those with LPRs can even
gain citizenship by undergoing a process called naturalization. This is a process in which a foreign individual
gains citizenship by fulfilling requirements set forth by
the US Congress in the Immigration and Nationality Act
(INA). There are limitations to being an LPR. You cannot vote, access all federal programs, make a home
outside of the country, or travel abroad for unlimited
amounts of time. US Citizenship and Immigration
Services (USCIS) must be notified of address changes or
criminal acts. If they've committed fraud to obtain their
citizenship or have been convicted of a criminal act, they
can be deported.

HOW UNDOCUMENTED PEOPLE ARRIVE IN THE UNITED STATES

Legal immigration takes a lot of time, money, and
patience. If immigrants cannot wait on or afford the
qualification process of becoming legal, they find alternative ways of entering the United States. These include
flying into the country and overstaying their travel visas,
or hiring professional smugglers known as coyotes.
Coyotes are paid thousands of dollars per person to
deliver immigrants across the Mexico/US border. They
are part of a large, but loose, network on both sides of

the border. They keep track of border agent schedules, use high-tech surveillance devices, and pay bribes to corrupt law enforcement to "look the other way." Immigrants are then taken into the United States by foot or vehicle. This can be very dangerous because of extreme temperatures, rugged terrain, or overstuffed vehicles. Once across the border, coyotes deliver immigrants to safe houses in big cities, such as Los Angeles, San Diego, or Phoenix. Immigrants then eat, shower, and change clothes before heading out again to destinations across the country. Payment is due upon delivery. If one cannot pay, he or she is returned or expected to work off the debt. This means caring for or driving other immigrants. It could also mean acting as a drug mule. If caught, immigrants are sent back

In a U.S. Border Patrol detention center in Arizona, posters warn of the dangers associated with hiring coyotes to help migrants sneak across the border.

across the border. Many try again until they are successful.

WHERE DO ILLEGAL IMMIGRANTS GO?

Pew Research Center notes that there are six states that "account for 60 percent of unauthorized immigrants—California, Texas, Florida, New York, New Jersey, and Illinois." However, the population is increasing in "Florida, Idaho, Maryland, Nebraska, New Jersey, Pennsylvania, and Virginia."

Big cities have historically offered more job opportunities. More recently, though, Midwestern and Southern states have been drawing larger immigration populations, especially as these locations have more low-skilled labor opportunities.

There are many myths regarding undocumented immigrants. Below are three:

MYTH
Immigrants drain the US economy.

FACT
"As producers and consumers, illegal immigrants enlarge the economic pie by at least $36 billion a year," says Alvaro Vargas Llosa of Forbes.com (2013). "That number would triple if they were legal—various studies point to a $1 trillion impact on GDP [Gross Domestic Product] in ten years."

MYTH
Undocumented immigrants do not pay taxes.

FACT
The 50-state study, "Undocumented Immigrants' State and Local Tax Contributions" (2016), by the Institute on Taxation and Economic Policy (ITEP) reports that the "11 million undocumented immigrants currently living in the United States collectively paid $11.64 billion in state and local taxes."

MYTH
Entering the United States illegally is not a criminal act.

FACT
According to US immigration laws, an undocumented immigrant who has illegally entered the country is subject to a criminal penalties. These include fines and/or jail time.

MYTHS AND FACTS

Many undocumented youth want to go to school. They know that an education can help them get a job, make a living, enjoy meaningful experiences, and gain a widespread network of interesting people. Because of *Plyler vs. Doe*, undocumented students have the right to go to school in the United States.

Approximately 1.7 million of undocumented youth in the Unites States are enrolled in elementary, middle, and high school, or have graduated or obtained a General Education Diploma (GED).

PLYLER V. DOE: THE RIGHT TO A PUBLIC EDUCATION

In 1982, the US Supreme Court ruled that the US Constitution guarantees *all* children—even undocumented youth—equal access to a free public education. This is the same right shared by US citizens and permanent residents. The case of *Plyler v. Doe* involved a 1975 Texas law. It withheld funds to educate undocumented children. School districts then reacted by preventing the enrollment of undocumented students, expelling them, or charging tuition. Tuition in Tyler, Texas, was $1,000 a year. Students who couldn't afford this were driven from the classroom almost immediately. The Mexican American Legal Defense and Educational Fund (MALDEF) filed a lawsuit, which was later paired with a

Sometimes undocumented immigrants are separated from their families. They risk coming to the United States illegally to reunite with loved ones. This could negatively affect their chance of receiving a green card.

If undocumented youths graduate, they'll be more likely to secure better careers, make more money, and contribute to the economy.

similar Houston-based lawsuit. The US Supreme Court claimed that the law violated the Equal Protection Clause of the Fourteenth Amendment. The American Civil Liberties Union (ACLU) notes the following in "School Is for Everyone: Celebrating *Plyler v. Doe*" (2012):

As the Court recognized, education was crucial to preventing a permanent underclass of undocumented immigrants in the United States and ensuring immigrants' future membership in society. Citing *Brown v. Board of Education*, the Court recognized that "denying these children a basic education" would "deny them the ability to live within the structure of our civic institutions, and foreclose any realistic possibility that they will contribute in even the smallest way to the progress of our Nation."

Plyler also set the stage for today's battles over higher education, as immigrant youth fight to defend their ability to enroll in colleges and universities; access in-state tuition, scholarships, and financial aid; and secure passage of the DREAM Act's path to citizenship for immigrants who came to the United States as children and graduate from high school.

ENSURING EDUCATIONAL SUCCESS

Even though every student has the right to attend school, some still do not. They might not be fluent in English, be afraid of discovery, or need to work to support their families. "Removing Barriers to Higher Education for Undocumented Students," an article from 2014, points out that "40 percent of undocumented young people ages 18 to 24 do not complete high school, compared with 8 percent of their US-born peers."

If you wish to get your high school diploma and move on to complete a professional certificate or degree, there are some things you can do to ensure your success. Work hard. Maintain a high grade point average (GPA). Stay connected to teachers and counselors who can offer support and resources. If possible, enroll in college prep courses. (You'll not only get college credit, but you also can use these to demonstrate a commitment to your education.) Do well on college entrance exams, such as the SAT or ACT. Fill in your schedule with volunteering and extracurricular activities at your school and in your community. These will set you apart from other applicants when applying to colleges and vocational schools.

TO SHARE OR NOT TO SHARE

Undocumented students are cautious about sharing their status with school authorities. This is understandable, as they do not want to be detained or deported. However, public schools are not permitted to disclose any personal information about its students. This includes immigration status. Also, schools are not allowed to deny admission to undocumented students, or treat them differently in order to determine status. Furthermore, school officials cannot inquire or require students, or their parents, to share their immigration status. Nor can they require students' Social Security numbers, which would expose their undocumented status.

Colleges, too, cannot report one's immigration status. They are limited by the Federal Education Rights and Privacy Act (FERPA), which applies to those schools that are funded by the US Department of Education. FERPA ensures that these universities do not release student information, including their undocumented status. Exceptions have to be very specific.

Court orders fall into this category. BestColleges.com reports the following:

Application advisors, admission officers, and financial aid counselors are not required by law to report undocumented students to the US Citizenship and Immigration Services (USCIS). What students tell their counselors and potential schools does not count as incriminating evidence against them, and their advisors may be able to point them to resources that will help them gain a temporary legal status through DACA (Deferred Action for Childhood Arrivals).

In 2012, President Obama announced his administration's efforts to stop deporting some young people who have arrived in the country as children of illegal immigrants.

LIVING THE DREAM ACT

The CollegeBoard.org report, "Young Lives on Hold," estimates that approximately 65,000 undocumented students graduate from US high schools annually. However, only 5 to 10 percent go to college. This can be due to a lack of finances, or to a fear of discovery during the application process. The Development, Relief and Education for Alien Minors (DREAM) Act is an attempt to remedy that.

Proposed in 2001, the DREAM Act was intended as a path to citizenship for those who entered the country when they were under sixteen years of age. The act, however, has been repeatedly rejected by Congress. There have been several versions over the years. In its present configuration, the DREAM Act takes six years to complete. Eligible applicants must be in school, have graduated or received a certificate of completion from high school, earned a GED, or have been an honorably discharged veteran of the Coast Guard or armed forces of the United States. Once the requirements are filled, the conditional residency can lead to permanent residency, which is an important aspect in acquiring US citizenship.

Although the DREAM Act has not yet been passed into law, a number of states have created their own versions. Qualifying criteria and benefits depend on the state. These state-based DREAM Acts do not lead to citizenship, but they do recognize the right of undocumented students to get a college education. Overall, they tend to include in-state tuition, and eligibility for scholarships and state financial aid. An example of a state-based

Part of becoming an independent member of society is becoming your own advocate. This means knowing your rights, asking for help, searching out community support, and pressing until you get the answers needed to take the next step. When considering the next step after high school, look for a school that has programs and resources devoted especially to undocumented students. This could be scholarships and student services programs. If faced with financing your higher education, talk with a guidance counselor, college admissions officer, or a financial aid representative. Present your situation, and ask them if they know of any resources that can help. Don't rely on school websites alone for the most current information. These sites may be in transition, and have yet to publish more updated policies, scholarships, and programs. Also, don't assume that school administrators fully know or understand their state's immigration policies. If you need to speak with their supervisor for more information, ask to set up a phone or in-person meeting. When filling out application forms, you may be required to include your Social Security number (SSN). Find out if this is actually needed. Oftentimes, it's just used to track students. Perhaps an alternative, such as a student identification number, could be used instead.

BECOME YOUR OWN ADVOCATE

scholarship is the Illinois Dream Fund Scholarship. Applicants for this scholarship must be a high school senior, have earned a GED, or be an undergraduate student with a 2.5–4.0 GPA. Eligibility requirements may vary from year to year.

PAYING FOR A COLLEGE EDUCATION

A college education is expensive, no matter one's legal status. Students have to fund their own education or qualify for financial aid, scholarships, grants, loans, and work study opportunities. Undocumented students are not eligible for federally funded financial aid. However, they may be eligible for state-funded financial aid. Eligibility depends on the state. Participating states include—but are not limited to—California, Minnesota, New Mexico, Texas, and Washington.

Free Money with Scholarships and Grants

Scholarships and grants are a popular way to cover the costs of tuition, books, and living expenses. They offer free money, as opposed to private loans that you have to pay back. Scholarships and grants vary, but many are merit-based. This means that applicants must prove academic excellence and/or community involvement. Merit-based scholarships are provided by private or public educational institutions, as well as community organizations. If you are interested in a particular scholarship, check to see if applicants must have citizenship or legal residency. Some do, and some don't. High school counselors can point you in the right direction. The Mexican American Legal Defense and Education Fund (MALDEF), United We Dream, and Educators for Fair Consideration (E4FC) lists scholarships and grants for undocumented undergraduate and graduate students. Nonprofit groups, school organizations, and the local chamber of commerce may also sponsor scholarships that are accessible to undocumented students.

COMPLETING THE ADMISSIONS APPLICATION

US colleges do not deny admission based on immigration status. However, it is important to be truthful when filling out admission forms. Acceptances can be revoked if the institution discovers that the information on the form has been falsified. To apply, you may be asked to include standardized test scores, high school transcripts, a completed application form, a letter of intent or personal statement, letters of recommendation from teachers, and application fees. Personal essays and interviews may also be required. This would be a great opportunity to share your story. Explain why you want to go to college, and what you plan to do upon graduation. Let schools know about the challenges you've overcome, and how these are only a small part of the whole you. Because, after all, you are more than your status.

You may also be asked about your country of citizenship. Applications in some states provide an "Other," "None of the Above," or "No Selection" option. Use one of these responses, even if you have DACA status. (DACA will be discussed in Chapters Three and Five.) If asked for a SSN, you may be able to skip this portion of

By law, schools cannot report your status, so this should not prevent you from accurately including all required information on your college and scholarship applications.

the application. Students are assigned a student identification number during the application process. If they attend the school, the student ID number will be used throughout their college experience.

CHAPTER 3

GETTING A JOB AS AN UNDOCUMENTED YOUTH

According to the Pew Research Center (2015), "Unauthorized immigrants make up 5.1 percent of the US labor force." Many cannot obtain permission in the form of a visa to legally work. This makes them vulnerable to unsafe, and perhaps unethical, work environments. They may believe that working in sweatshops or drug and/or human trafficking is the only way to earn a living. If undocumented workers are able to secure employment in legitimate industries, such as agriculture, construction, mining, and logging, they may find themselves working in unsafe environments without little recourse. They may fear that the employer will report them to the authorities. Or they may not have the English fluency to express themselves throughout the reporting process. Still, they may not know that employers are required by law to provide a safe work environment for all employees. If you, or someone you know, is working in such an environment, seek the assistance of an advocacy organization. You may even want to connect with an attorney to find out what options are available. But

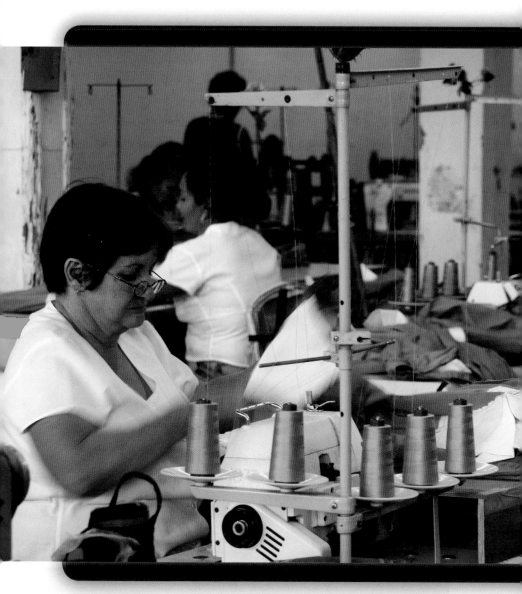

If undocumented individuals want to work, they may find it difficult to work a legitimate job. They may be forced to work long hours for little pay in order to support themselves and their family.

whatever you do, do not be tempted to get false documents. These are considered a violation of immigration law, and if caught, could ruin any chance of gaining lawful status in the United States.

THE EMPLOYER'S BUSINESS

It is illegal for employers to knowingly hire undocumented employees. According to the US Department of Justice, "Title 8 U.S.C. § 1324a(a)(1)(A) makes it unlawful for any person or other entity to hire, recruit, or refer for a fee, for employment in the United States an alien knowing the alien is an unauthorized alien..." In turn, employers are obligated to verify every employee's identity and employment authorization. Sometimes they do, and sometimes they don't. If employers are caught hiring undocumented people—knowing that they are not authorized to

B&H Photo Video employees protested dangerous and discriminatory working conditions in New York City. More than 100 workers took part in the protest, hoping to make a difference.

NETWORK YOUR WAY TO PROFESSIONAL SUCCESS

If you choose to work for yourself, you can build your business by networking. Networking is a method of connecting with individuals and professional organizations in order to expand your circles, learn about new opportunities, and build a professional reputation in your field. In this case, you can network with undocumented individuals, as well as beyond the undocumented community. Consider the local Rotary Club, chamber of commerce, business networking groups, social programs, and churches. You may be able to attend conferences, lectures, social events, and workshops they host throughout the year. While attending these events, bring business cards to share. Effective networking is about helping each other, so there's no need to be shy. Everyone is there to network, so let them know what you have to offer. You can make your own business cards or have them professionally printed. Choose a design that matches your personality and professionalism. For example, if you're a dog walker, add paw prints for a visual reminder. Be sure to include your name, contact information, and social media platforms that you use for business. As the event continues, you'll likely gather a collection of cards given by other entrepreneurs. Follow up with a friendly "It was nice to meet you" email or phone call to keep the conversation going. Keep in mind that networking is not limited to business alone. It is a good skill to have in social and educational settings, too.

work in the United States—fines could be assessed. These range from $375 to $3,200 per unauthorized employee. Fines go up, and prison time could be ordered, for ongoing illegal hiring practices.

YOUR RIGHTS IN THE WORKPLACE

It is important to know your rights, so that you're not taken advantage of in the workplace. If you are employed, you have the right to work in an environment that is safe and free from sexual harassment, abuse, and exploitation. You have the right to receive a paycheck, and be paid for overtime when legally required. If working conditions are poor, you have the right to join a union. And if there isn't a union, you can create your own to improve working conditions. Should you get an on-the-job injury, you also have the right to workers' compensation. This could depend on the state in which you live. Unemployment insurance is not available to undocumented employees in most states because they are not legally supposed to be working and do not qualify. This is reserved for those who are legal, able, and want to work.

THE ENTREPRENEURIAL SPIRIT

Thousands of small businesses in the United States are owned by undocumented immigrants with an entrepreneurial spirit. They open everything from restaurants and farmer's markets to lawn maintenance and construction companies. They are able to do this because "federal and state laws often do not require proof of immigration status for an individual to go into business for him or herself and receive payment for goods or services," notes E4FC's "Life After College: A Guide for Undocumented Students." Duarte Geraldino of Aljazeera.America.com explains:

> Using a birth certificate or some form of official foreign ID (passport, military, or state identification), an immigrant can apply for an Individual Taxpayer Identification Number (ITIN). With the ITIN in hand, he can apply for an Employer Identification Number. Section 7b of this form asks for a Social Security number or—and this is how it's all possible—an ITIN number. That's it. Once he's granted these IDs, the Internal Revenue Service considers him the owner of a legal US company. Yet, because owning a business does not change immigration status, the US government can still deport him at any time.

Some undocumented immigrants, known as sole proprietors, establish much smaller-scale businesses. They teach piano, walk dogs, write blog articles, clean houses, bake cupcakes, or tutor children. They manage their own schedule, use their own tools and supplies, hire employees, and choose with whom they service. Sole proprietors keep what they earn but are required to pay personal income tax on their profits. Instead of a SSN, they use an ITIN. Fees for business name registration and business licenses may apply, depending on the county and state in which they work.

Working Options for Undocumented Youth

Two options exist for undocumented youth who want to work in the United States. The first is DACA. It is an executive branch program, put into place by President Barack Obama in 2012. It temporarily protects qualifying undocumented students, or DREAMers, from deportation. Those with DACA status can get a job or internship, have a driver's license (depending on their state), open a bank account, and gain access to healthcare. To qualify, undocumented youth must have come to the United States under the age of sixteen, and must have been under age thirty-one as of June 15, 2012. Educational requirements are also in place, requiring DREAMers to either be enrolled in school (or another qualifying educational program), or have earned a high school diploma or GED. While DACA gives legal presence, it doesn't grant a green card or US citizenship. DACA sponsorship doesn't extend to immediate family members, a spouse, or children. It also doesn't allow the recipient to sponsor relatives. DACA is good for two years and can be renewed.

The second option for undocumented youth who want to work in the United States is Special Immigrant Juvenile Status (SIJS). It is limited to those who have undergone—and can prove—abuse, neglect, or abandonment by a parent(s). Proof must be given by court order, and is required to show that it is not in the youth's best interest to return to the country of origin. To be eligible, you do not need to be enrolled in school or hold a high school diploma or GED. Nor do you need to have been in the United States for a specific amount of time. Government benefits, including federal student financial aid, are available to those with SIJS status. Plus, it is a pathway toward lawful permanent residence and eventually US citizenship. The application process and limitations of both DACA and SIJS are noted in Chapter Five.

While the Constitution guarantees that all citizens have equal protection under the law, many born to undocumented immigrants do not feel as if they have access to the benefits of citizenship.

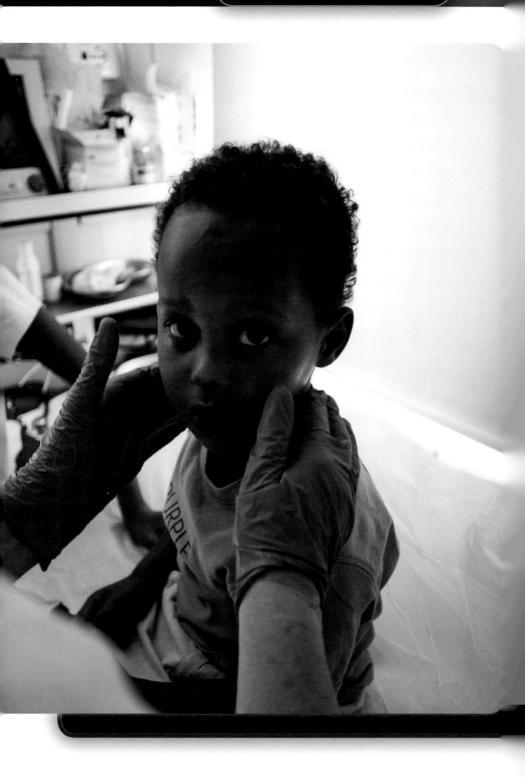

An internship will give you on-the-job skills, which can lead to more opportunities, a broader professional network, clarity on a career choice, and a brighter future.

GET HANDS-ON LEARNING WITH AN INTERNSHIP

If you are eligible, internships are a great way to "try on" a work- or research-related position in a particular industry. They are temporary positions in a company, advocacy group, or nonprofit organization. Sometimes they offer class credit, a paying wage, a scholarship, and/or a stipend that isn't dependent on one's status.

Internships give hands-on experience, which is especially appealing to admissions committees and employers. You will learn more about your field of interest and have the chance to decide if it's one in which you'd like to continue pursuing. Internships provide additional skills, which can advance your chances of getting your foot in the door with that particular organization. They also give you a chance to practice your networking skills, which is a good way to discover jobs that aren't publicized. Plus, you'll make new friends with people who share your professional interests. To find out more about internships for which you qualify, connect with your teacher, guidance counselor, or academic advisor.

CHAPTER 4

Undocumented immigrants often live in constant fear of being deported. This can be especially scary for their children, who dread the thought of being deported to a country they may not know or remember. They try to blend in, not wanting to attract attention to themselves or their families. Plus, they have the stresses associated with feeling different from their native-born or documented peers. Their language, clothing, food, manners, music, beliefs, values, and practices may be strikingly different, which can make friendships difficult to create. Outside pressures, such as discrimination and racial profiling, can be frustrating to deal with and challenging to overcome. But facing one's fears, with a positive attitude and willingness to overcome, can make all the difference in achieving the goal of permanent residency in the United States.

WHAT ARE DISCRIMINATION AND RACIAL PROFILING?

Discrimination is common for immigrants with legal status or not. In fact, they may experience it for the first time in the United States. Discrimination can take place at work or in school, but it can also occur at the grocery store, in the dog park, and at the bus station. It can bring about feelings of not belonging and of being a second-class individual. Mental health issues can arise, including stress, anxiety, and depression. Victims of discrimination could turn to substance abuse and thoughts of suicide.

Racial profiling takes this treatment to the next level. It creates a profile that targets a particular group of people based on their outer appearance, as well as ethnicity, race, or religion. Government officials have used racial profiling when tracking criminal activity. In such cases, their search has focused on the

Community organizations can help undocumented immigrants get the resources they need to manage their emotions and deal with their circumstances.

Understanding the Stress and Anxiety of Being Undocumented

Stress is that overwhelming feeling you have when faced with the pressures of living as an undocumented individual. Your heart races, your breathing quickens, and a burst of energy surges through your body—all symptoms of the fight-or-flight stress response kicking in. Your body thinks it's in danger, which is normal. But if it doesn't calm down, anxiety can set it. This is a reaction to stress levels. If anxiety continues, it can turn into a condition called an anxiety disorder. This disorder disrupts your life, making it hard to function normally. Symptoms include muscle tension, nausea, heart palpitations, an inability to remain calm, cold/sweaty hands or feet, disrupted sleep, and feelings of panic. Then there's post-traumatic stress disorder (PTSD). It is brought on by a single or series of traumatic, life-threatening events. These experiences can include overwhelming difficulties in one's country of origin, coming to the United States, and living in a constant state of high alert. PTSD is diagnosed by a mental health professional.

To cope, undocumented immigrants may turn to their families or community for help. If either of these two are lacking, they may turn to dangerous coping solutions, such as substance abuse, violence, illegal activity, and thoughts of suicide. If you are experiencing any of these, or know someone who is, consult a counselor or medical professional.

Professional help is always a good idea if you're dealing with overwhelming and insurmountable emotions. Consider working with a therapist if you think you have an anxiety disorder. Psychotherapy, also known as talk therapy, may be used alone or in combination with medications, such as antidepressants, anti-anxiety medication, or sedatives. Treatment for PTSD is a bit different. It uses one or more forms of psychotherapy to improve symptoms. Medications may be a part of the treatment plan. There are three forms of psychotherapy used for PTSD: cognitive therapy, exposure therapy, and eye movement desensitization and reprocessing (EMDR). Cognitive therapy helps you to recognize how your thinking keeps you stuck. Exposure therapy helps you to face your fears. EMDR partners exposure therapy with guided eye movements to improve your reaction to traumatic memories.

(continued on the next page)

Regular exercise helps you to work through stress and anxiety. It causes your body to release feel-good chemicals known as endorphins.

(continued from the previous page)

There are also some things you can do on your own. Slow your mind and body with daily meditation. Get plenty of exercise, eat healthy foods, drink lots of water, and get a good night's sleep. Laugh often, stay thankful, and look for opportunities to give to others in need. Then be sure to find a trusted ally with whom you can share your thoughts and feelings. A friend, teacher, or counselor could be a good choice. And don't forget that there are advocacy groups that offer 24-hour hotlines, as well as one-on-one or group counseling options.

generalization rather than the behavior. These generalizations create an atmosphere of fear and anxiety for immigrants who fear deportation.

BECOMING "AMERICANIZED"

Undocumented immigrants often feel pressure to become "Americanized" whether they want to or not. They may feel that they have to change everything about themselves, from language and music to clothing and faith systems, to fit in. This can be stressful and is worth discussing among family members and trusted adults.

It's also important to note that undocumented youth may want to become Americanized, if they aren't already. Their peers are likely citizens and permanent residents, and they want to socialize with them by sharing common interests. They are quick to Americanize. This starts with language, fashion, food, and entertainment. Gender identity and roles, faith systems, relationship building, and professional interests soon follow. This may cause a gap between them and their immigrant parents and grandparents who want to hold on to their cultural identity and values. Youths may find it hard to have certain customs in public, and other customs at home. They may feel that their parents don't understand, and this can greatly effect communication and trust.

Furthermore, immigrant youth may experience role reversal. They will have to become translators for non-English-speaking relatives. Or they will have to be cultural teachers, helping family members navigate popular culture. If you can relate, seek counseling services that assist immigrants with adapting to a new culture. One thing to keep in mind is that both cultures offer value, and a balance of the new and old can make the transition easier for the entire family.

The Hard Facts About ICE

The United States' immigration policy is enforced by three entities: US Customs and Border Protection (CBP), US Citizenship and Immigration Services (USCIS), and Immigration and Customs Enforcement (ICE). CBP is responsible for preventing terrorists and their weapons from coming into the country. USCIS processes petitions for immigrant visas and naturalization, as well as asylum and refugee applications. ICE works to identify and apprehend what ICE.gov notes as, "criminal aliens and

Immigrants might become fluent in the native language of their adopted nation or even adopt some local customs, while still maintaining their cultural identity.

other priority aliens located in the United States." It also detains and removes "those individuals appre-hended in the interior of the United States as well as those apprehended by CBP officers and agents patrol-ling our nation's borders."

ICE uses a variety of methods to seek out undocumented individu-als. They conduct raids, sweeping through workplaces and communi-ties, and make random stops, checking passerby for legal docu-mentation. Local and law enforcement groups assist ICE in the endeavors. If it is discovered that someone is unlawfully present in the Unites States during a minor traffic stop, the person is taken into custody, and ICE is contacted. ICE may file a "detainer," which allows the person to be held until an interview can be conducted. This determines one's immigration status and whether or not to begin removal (deportation) proceedings. One can only be detained on ICE's behalf for a maximum of forty-eight hours. If this time passes without being taken into custody, the person can be released. ICE doesn't always put arrestees into custody. Those with a family, without a criminal history, or who have already a filed case for relief from removal, are often allowed to go home. Deportation attempts may continue, but no time will be spent in an immigration jail. They may, however, be ordered to wear an electronic monitoring device (EMD) on their ankle. For those who are detained, they are transferred to an ICE detention center. These differ from what is thought of as ordinary jails, and are often located in other states.

WHAT HAPPENS IN REMOVAL PROCEEDINGS

Removal proceedings begin with a Notice to Appear (NTA). It is an official accusation against a person who is unlawfully present in the United States. The NTA details the legal reasons why it is believed that one is in the country illegally and puts that individual on notice that an immigration court date has been set. If an order of removal has previously been given, however, the immigrant doesn't have a right to any additional hearings. Deportation may follow.

The Rights of Detainees

If you are detained, you have the right to make a free, local phone call. This is often made to a family member, friend, employer, or immigration attorney. Detainees also have the right to speak with the consulate of their country of origin. The consulate can possibly assist by contacting your family members, and securing an immigration attorney for your case. Always share your location and alien registration number, also known as the "A number," in the event relatives and legal representation need to find you. It is not uncommon for detainees to be moved on the spot to another detention center.

You also have the right to receive paperwork that you can understand. If not, an interpreter can help you review the forms. Do not sign anything that is difficult to understand or that you don't agree with. Contact an immigration attorney—or even the consulate of your country of origin—prior to signing anything. You have the right to present your case to an immigration judge not associated with ICE. Keep in mind, though, that this doesn't always happen. "Immigration courts are severely backlogged and under-resourced," noted the American Immigration Council in 2015. It goes on to explain that between 2005 and 2015, immigration court backlogs grew by 247 percent. By the end of September 2015, there were 456,216 cases, and the average pending time for a deportation case was 643 days. According to Nolo.com's Christine Galvan, "Removal proceedings can be lengthy, sometimes taking years to complete. As long as you do not have a prior order of removal, nor sign agreement to your deportation or accept voluntary departure, you will not be immediately deported just because you are caught." Voluntary departure is leaving the country, at your own expense, without an order of deportation going on your immigration record. This typically follows an unsuccessful argument in court to not be deported and is approved by an immigration judge. Undocumented immigrants sometimes choose voluntary departure because it doesn't bar them from legally returning at a later date, provided they qualify for a new visa or green card application.

Paying a Bond

While in immigration custody, a deportation official will determine if a bond should be paid. This is known as bail, and it allows you to be released to your US-based home, while removal proceedings are taking place. When considering a bond, the official takes into account the chance that you might miss immigration hearings or become a

Guatemalan immigrants make a free phone call to loved ones after arriving on a deportation flight from the United States to Guatemala City, Guatemala.

Because of the deportation of their undocumented parents, thousands of youth live with friends or relatives, on the streets, or in the foster care system.

danger to the community. A bond can cost up to $25,000, depending on the case. If a bond is too expensive or refused, the individual has the right to request a reconsideration by an immigration judge.

What Happens to the Children?

Among those detained and arrested for their immigrant status are parents with unlawful status. Sometimes they are detained for a few hours, and sometimes for several months, or even years. This is particularly hard on their children, who do not know if and when they'll have their parents back home.

These children often stay with friends or relatives. If no one is available to care of them in the long-term, they may be placed in the child welfare system to live in a foster or group home. It is not uncommon for parents to be released early in order to care for their children. They will likely have to pay the bond, wear an EMD, and stay in the area until their deportation cases are resolved. There are cases, too, in which parents opt for voluntary departure. They are permitted to spend time with their families before leaving the country. This gives them the opportunity to make arrangements for their children: to take them along, or leave them with a second parent or relative. But keep in mind that, depending on the circumstances, deportation can be a long, drawn-out process. Just because someone's been ordered to be deported doesn't mean it's the end. The ruling can be delayed, appealed, and even overturned.

CHAPTER 5

Undocumented immigrants often live in the shadows, hiding their unlawful status. And while there is no direct path to citizenship for undocumented immigrants, there are some ways to get on a legal path. Please note that each option has unique qualifications, timelines, and associated fees.

GETTING A GREEN CARD

As mentioned previously, a Legal Permanent Resident (LPR) card, or green card, is given to qualifying immigrants. It gives the holder the right to live and work in the United States. However, undocumented immigrants who apply for a green card risk discovery and deportation. To work around this, you'll have to leave the country, visit a foreign consulate, and apply for permanent residency. This will take some time, years even, depending on factors such as your age and the length of time you have been in the United States illegally. Consult with an immigration attorney to determine what other eligibility standards might apply for your specific case. You can also request an estimation of how long you'll have to wait before returning to the United States.

NONIMMIGRANT VISAS

There are many types of visas, but the T nonimmigrant status (T visa) and the U nonimmigrant status (U visa) are often accessible for qualifying undocumented individuals.

T Nonimmigrant Status

Human traffickers prey on the poor, unemployed, marginalized, and unconnected from the strength and safety of strong social networks. They promise money, jobs, housing, and connections in return for working in inhumane conditions. Victims get stuck in this arrangement and are too afraid to speak up. The T nonimmigrant status— also known as T visa—protects victims who help with the investigation and prosecution of human trafficking cases. Eligible individuals must be in the United States because of human trafficking, and must cooperate with law enforcement and

If an immigrant comes to the United States illegally, he or she may face consequences when later applying for a green card or immigration benefits.

Fear, stress, and anxiety can run high for those who live in the United States illegally. It is important to recognize these feelings, and figure out what can be done to address them.

prosecutors. Or the eligible individual must be under the age of eighteen years old. Family members who qualify may also be eligible to apply for benefits.

U Nonimmigrant Status

The U nonimmigrant status (or U visa) is a part of the Victims of Trafficking and Violence Prevention Act. It provides protection for immigrants who have suffered physical or mental abuse due to a qualifying crime. These crimes include abusive sexual contact, domestic violence, incest, kidnapping, murder, and sexual assault. Like the T visa, the U visa requires victims to work with law enforcement. Any leads must advance the investigation or prosecution of qualifying criminal activity. The U visa application requires a certifying statement, known as a Form I-918 Supplement B. It is given by law enforcement or sometimes by a judge or representative from child protective services. US visa recipients gain lawful status in the country, are able to work, and can apply for a green card in some cases. Qualifying family members may also apply for benefits.

Non-LPR Cancellation of Removal

The Non-LPR Cancellation of Removal allows undocumented immigrants in the middle of removal proceedings to request a cancellation of the removal and to be granted a green card. This request is made to the immigration judge. Immigration judges have a lot of

Immigrants can gain legal permission if they are highly trained and have a job offer by a US employer, are seeking asylum, reuniting with family, or have won the green card lottery.

freedom when making application decisions. However, they are limited to approving 4,000 cancellation applications from non-LPRs (those without green cards) per year. To be eligible, you have to have been continually present in the country for a minimum of ten years. Plus, your deportation would need to cause "exceptional and extremely unusual hardship" to your relatives who are US citizens or LPRs. Examples may include a severely sick child who can't get adequate medical care in the country of origin, or an English-speaking tween who doesn't speak the language of his country of origin and is without a reliable support system. In addition to "exceptional and extremely unusual hardship," an undocumented immigrant needs to demonstrate "good moral character." This means that you're honest and sincere, and haven't violated particular laws or been convicted of specific crimes. Keep in mind that an immigration judge has a lot of liberty when it comes to approving or denying the application, even if all of the requirements have been met. To make your case as favorable as possible, consult an immigration attorney.

ASYLUM STATUS

Asylum status provides legal protection for those who fled persecution in their home country. Asylum means that you are applying within US borders. You are required to prove that you were persecuted and that you will be persecuted if you return. The persecution must be due to participation within a particular social group, nationality, political opinion, race, or religion. You must be present to apply, and you must prove that you cannot or will not return to your home country. The application is sent to USCIS, and an interview will follow. If approved, you can apply for a work permit, followed by applying for a green card one year later. The asylum seeker's spouse and children are also eligible to apply for a green card if they were admitted to the United States as asylum seekers. If the application is denied, removal proceedings will likely begin.

VIOLENCE AGAINST WOMEN ACT (VAWA)

Violence Against Women Act (VAWA) is a federal law that protects victims of domestic abuse by a US citizen or permanent resident. Qualifying victims, such as a youth, parent, or current/former spouse of the offender, can apply for a green card without needing their abuser to file for immigration benefits on their behalf. Eligibility is based on the ability to prove that the victim is in or has had a relationship with the offender. They must also have good moral character, have lived or currently live with the offender, and are indeed a victim. Those who want to apply can complete and submit the application forms without the help of an immigration attorney. Forms can be found at USCIS.gov. If the application is approved, the qualifier and children can apply for a work permit.

APPLYING FOR DACA AND SIJS

As mentioned in Chapter Three, DACA and SIJS allow undocumented youths to live, work, and attend school in the United States. In some cases, undocumented youth are eligible for both. DACA offers deferred action to those who meet the age and entrance date restrictions noted in Chapter Three. Eligibility is not lost as qualifying youth age. Applying for DACA is a one-step process that can be done by the applicant. There is no deadline, but this is subject to change based on legislative changes. The DACA application process does not interfere with other applications that you may have in the works for immigration benefits. Also, information about any undocumented relatives does not need to be included. All you need is documentation that proves you've been living in the United States since June 15, 2007, until the time of your application. USCIS reviews the entire duration, so it's a good idea to include as much documentation as possible. Plan to pay a fee and to hear back about your application within a few months. If the DACA application is accepted, you must remain in the country while the deferred action is in effect. If it is rejected, you might be placed in removal proceedings. Although there isn't an appeal process, you can file a new request. DACA lasts for two years and is renewable every two years. Renewal is not possible for those who are a threat to public or national safety. It is also not renewable for those who have been convicted of a felony, a significant misdemeanor (domestic violence, DUI/DWI, unlawful

Consider the following questions when searching for a qualified, experienced immigration attorney:

1. What is your experience in practicing immigration law and/or deportation law?

2. Have you worked on any cases that are similar to mine?

3. If I hired you, what steps would you take now and later?

4. What should I do or give to help you win my case?

5. What is your preferred method of communication?

6. What is your rate, and how much should I expect to pay at the end of this process?

7. What is the expected timeline for resolution?

8. Besides you, who else will be working on my case?

9. What are my chances of a successful outcome?

10. Will you provide written documentation of everything you will do for my case?

10 GREAT QUESTIONS TO ASK AN IMMIGRATION ATTORNEY

possession of a firearm, etc.), or three or more non-significant misdemeanors. For help with the DACA application process, connect with national organizations. OwntheDream.org, for example, has a toll-free hotline for DACA questions: (844) 411-DACA.

SIJS offers an employment authorization card, the chance to get a green card, and possibly US citizenship. They can also apply for government benefits, access federal student financial aid, get a driver's license (depending on the state), and even serve in the US military. However, qualifying applicants must be victims of abuse, neglect, or abandonment. A state court order—to be entered before your eighteenth birthday—must prove mistreatment and that staying in the country is in your best interest. You do need not be enrolled in school, hold a high school diploma or GED, or have been in the country for a particular time period. Keep in mind, however, that to apply for SIJS means sharing information about undocumented relatives. Work with an immigration attorney to complete the entire USCIS application process. It is complicated and should be finalized before you are twenty-one years old. Once a SIJS is granted, the holder is prohibited from sponsoring either parent for a green card, even if one parent was not abusive.

LEGALLY SPEAKING

From time to time, state and federal immigration laws change. Stay up on current legislation by staying informed. If and when you need legal advice or representation, contact a licensed attorney with a Board of Immigration Appeals (BIA) accredited agency or a BIA accredited representative (non-attorney). Either can represent you before USCIS and immigration courts. If you choose to work with an attorney, you might want to consider working with a child advocacy attorney. They often work pro bono. You can find a list of child advocacy attorneys through the National Association of Counsel for Children (NACC).

While searching for an attorney, always ask friends and community members for referrals. You want to find a professional who has won a lot of immigration cases that were similar to yours. Plus, referrals will help you avoid immigration scams with people posing as *notarios*. These are people who pose as immigration consultants in order to get paid. They take advantage of people in need, capitalizing on the confusion associated with *notario* and a notary public. A *notario* in Mexico is a legal profession. But in the United States, a notary public is not an attorney. This person is only authorized to witness and authenticate documents, administer oaths, and perform official acts. Latino immigrants often do not know the difference, and can get pulled into a situation that sounds too good to be true. If you suspect an immigration scam, report it to law enforcement or to the Federal Trade Commission (877-FTC-HELP).

If you think you have a legitimate attorney that you'd like to work with, have him or her review your

Even if you think your case is fairly straight-forward, the help of an immigration attorney can be effective if you have highly technical applications to complete.

documents before giving advice. Be forthcoming and deliver all of the requested information in a timely manner. The legal process can be unpredictable. However, your attorney should give you an idea of how long it will take. If you're paying for services, ask for a breakdown of the charges in case there are ways to minimize the cost. Request a retainer agreement before making a payment. This is a contract that details legal services and costs. Read it carefully, and make sure that you understand every element. Then get a copy of everything your attorney (or BIA accredited representative) files. Finally, stay informed about your case.

Even if you think your case is fairly straight-forward, the help of an immigration attorney can be effective if you have highly technical applications to complete.

documents before giving advice. Be forthcoming and deliver all of the requested information in a timely manner. The legal process can be unpredictable. However, your attorney should give you an idea of how long it will take. If you're paying for services, ask for a breakdown of the charges in case there are ways to minimize the cost. Request a retainer agreement before making a payment. This is a contract that details legal services and costs. Read it carefully, and make sure that you understand every element. Then get a copy of everything your attorney (or BIA accredited representative) files. Finally, stay informed about your case.

CHAPTER 6

How We Can Help Each Other

Undocumented immigrants often feel like outsiders, uncertain of where to turn for help and support. But most communities are filled with people who want to help you gain the knowledge and resources you need to succeed in the United States.

The Courage to Share and Trust

It takes courage to share your story and to trust those beyond your inner circle, especially when you need help. If you're experiencing difficulty of any kind, ask for help. Don't remain silent. You have the right to ask for help, no matter your status. And there are people out there who want to help. Search out those whom you trust. Maybe a teacher, counselor, social worker, or youth pastor can help with issues such as trouble fitting in, bullying, learning English, juggling schoolwork, or coping with issues at home. Plus, they may know of local, state, and national programs that can help you and your family. Give them the chance to listen and lend a helping hand. They want you to succeed in all areas of your life.

What to Do in the Event of...

If ICE comes to your door, make sure they present a signed warrant. Do not let ICE officials enter without a signed warrant. The signed warrant should be slid under the door for verification. It's unlikely they will come to your home if you haven't been convicted of a crime. This is due to a large number of cases, and a lack of time and resources to address them all.

Keep in mind that anything you say can be used against you in a court of law. So plead the Fifth Amendment, which means that you can't testify against yourself. Remain silent until you can talk with an immigration attorney. This goes for signing paperwork. Do not sign anything, including a voluntary departure document agreeing to be removed from the country. A good rule of thumb is to not sign any paperwork before speaking with an immigration attorney.

If a loved one has been detained, find out if he or she has been transferred to a different facility. This is a common practice, and can happen without much notice. Get as much information as you can, and encourage your loved one not to sign anything until an attorney can offer some advice. Attorneys may be expensive, but according to the American Immigration Council, "State and national studies continue to show the correlation between representation and successful case outcomes. A 2011 study of New York immigration courts found that people in detention facing deportation were six times more likely to obtain relief if they had a lawyer." Perhaps

Besides their status, undocumented students have the same hopes and dreams as legal students. And today there are ways and resources to ensure that those dreams become a reality.

a case can be made against removal. Or maybe your relative has a right to a green card. And if a crime was committed, maybe it's not bad enough to warrant deportation.

BE YOUR OWN ADVOCATE

Don't be afraid to protect your rights. Educate yourself so you know what you have, and then speak up if they are jeopardized. Be ready to educate others who may not know or understand state and federal immigration policies, even if they are school administrators. Then connect with community and church groups that work with undocumented youth and immigrant communities. If you dream of going to college, talk to school officials who may be able to work with you. If your state doesn't have a DREAM Act, perhaps your school offers merit scholarships that are not tied to federal funding. You can also look into E4FC, National Immigration Law Center (NILC), and United We Dream for scholarships and grants.

START YOUR OWN DREAMER ORGANIZATION

If you don't have a DREAMer organization in your school or community, start your own. Give

Students from the East Los Angeles community group InnerCity Struggle peacefully protest against proposed legislation that would strengthen the enforcement of immigration laws and tighten border security.

undocumented students a safe place in which to give and receive encouragement, support, and advice. It will take time, work, and persistence, but the payoff will be rewarding for you and others. Connect with administrators for the best way to begin. Secure a meeting time and location. Use flyers, posters, and an online presence to invite students, parents, faculty, and community members. Then schedule a wide range of speaking topics and activities to help undocumented students and allies. For ongoing ideas, support, and resources, look to United We Dream, a national immigrant youth-led organization.

SHARE THE POSSIBILITIES

Gather together students (and their parents) to discuss the educational and legislative possibilities that await DREAMers. Encourage students to stay in school, and point out the benefits of achieving a higher education at a community college, trade school, or four-year university. Invite guest students to share how they found scholarships and raised funds. Organize a college application drive, in which students complete their forms with the help of a counselor. Then consider starting a scholarship fund to help members pursue their educational goals. Discuss pro-immigrant legislation at the local, state, and federal levels. Dispel any myths that undocumented youths and their allies may have. Educate them and others about the benefits of the federal DREAM Act.

Educate, Inspire, and Motivate

Invite speakers to share their own experiences, and provide helpful services. Consider former undocumented students, immigrant faculty members, health and wellness professionals, and immigration attorneys. They can cover a wide variety of topics, such as navigating community and state college systems, applying for a visa, and avoiding immigration scams. Organizations such as E4FC have community educators that present college, career, and citizenship workshops and presentations for students at your school.

Stay Active

Keep your members learning and sharing. Host workshops to cover DACA, childcare, employment, financial literacy, healthcare, and legal services. Write formal letters and emails to local representatives. Maintain your social media platforms with encouragement, testimonials, upcoming events, and immigration news. Come up with response plans if you or someone you love is detained.

Team Up Today

Team up with other DREAMer youth and advocacy groups. Work together to plan special events in community centers, churches, libraries, and law centers. Examples include legal assistance workshops, and weekly discussions. Talk about the things that are most important to undocumented individuals and families. Popular topics range from pursuing college; the college enrollment/application process; and communication skills among students, parents, school authorities, and community leaders. You can even connect your group with other advocacy organizations on a local, state, and national level. And take your support to the next level with community outreach. Former undocumented youth can serve as role models, inspiring others with their success stories. By teaming up with others, you will spread awareness more quickly than you could on your own. Plus, members will feel more connected to a larger community, and networking opportunities will develop.

Undocumented youths who have lived in the United States for most of their lives want to be recognized for what they are—Americans. They want to be able to do and be anything they want.

KNOW YOUR RIGHTS (AND YES, YOU HAVE RIGHTS)

Even though the presence of undocumented immigrants in the United States is considered illegal, they do have rights according to the US Constitution. A provision of the Fourteenth Amendment states, "No state shall . . . deprive any person of life, liberty or property, without due process of law; nor deny to any person within its jurisdiction the equal protection of the laws." These rights include the right to defend yourself against deportation, the right to a hearing before an immigration judge, the right to a jury trial, and the right to defend yourself against the charges. You also have the right to file a lawsuit in federal court, including a discrimination suit. Depending on the state, you may even be able to sue in a state court. According to Ilona Bray of Lawyers.com, other amendments to the Constitution "protect undocumented immigrants against unlawful search and seizure by law enforcement authorities (without probable cause and a warrant for such an action) and against self-incrimination."

"International human rights apply to all human beings, regardless of immigration status," notes LoveIsRespect.org. Everyone has the right to ask for help from law enforcement, community service providers, and school officials without fear. The website goes on to note:

> Sometimes, your parent's immigration status may also get in the way of looking for help, for fear that your parents may be exposed or "found out." For example, if you're in a dating violence situation and your partner knows that your parents are undocumented, they may threaten you by telling

you that they will call the police and turn your parents in. Or if their parents are undocumented, they may tell you that you can't get help because it'll put your partner's family at risk. Remember, you have the right to seek help regardless of your documentation status. If you are fearful or unsure about what to do, contact a peer advocate as your first step.

BE A FRIEND AND ALLY

If you're not an immigrant but know someone who is, you can help by offering your friendship and support. Simply reach out and spend the time getting to know one another. Never ask your friend to self-identify, and avoid making assumptions. Always show respect, and be mindful of the language you use when discussing immigration-related issues. Instead of using terms like "illegal" and "alien," say "undocumented" and "DREAMer." If your friend decides to confide in you, listen without judgment. Encourage him or her to establish an identity that is different from the stigma and stereotypes surrounding an undocumented status. And whatever you do, avoid sharing your friend's status with others. This information is not yours to share. Lastly, and most important, encourage your friend to keep dreaming and take action, as anything is possible!

BECOME A PEER ADVOCATE

Whether you are undocumented or not, you can become an advocate for undocumented immigrants in your community. Keep yourself educated about the challenges facing undocumented youths. Support the DREAM Act and other related legislation in social circles. Become active in a support group for undocumented students and families. Join advocacy organizations that advise, support, offer programming, and connect those in need. If none of these exist, start your own. And if you see that someone

Make a difference in the life of another by becoming a friend and ally. Share a laugh, go for an adventure, hang out at a coffee shop, and be willing to talk things through.

is being bullied or abused because of their ethnicity, race, culture, language, or beliefs, do something about it. Don't be afraid to stand up for them, as two is always better than one.

If it continues or becomes violent, talk to someone in authority, such as parents, teachers, school administrators, security guards, and bus drivers. Together, you can devise a plan to stop bullying and educate others on the importance of acceptance and advocacy.

LIVE BEYOND YOUR IMMIGRATION STATUS

Don't let your immigration status dominate your thoughts. Seek outlets to distract your mind, relieve stress, and lift the spirits. Get involved in meaningful experiences, such as volunteering at an animal shelter, serving at a food bank, or tutoring a neighbor in math. This will let you build new social networks, minimize feelings of isolation, and build your understanding of US culture.

If you're having trouble getting beyond your situation, seek outside help. Perhaps a therapist could help you identify what is causing the problem and ways of coping with it. There are different types of therapists, including counselors, social workers, psychologists, and psychiatrists. Each has a unique way of tackling problems, but they are all well versed in listening, and helping you to deal with intense and difficult emotions. During your appointment—or series of appointments—you may be asked to come in to the therapist's office alone or with an adult. The choice is yours. The conversation space is safe, and anything that you share will be kept confidential. Your therapist will likely offer unique perspectives and coping solutions to help you release stress and focus on the positivity in your life. Appointments last about forty-five to sixty minutes.

Keep Moving Forward

Despite the many risks undocumented immigrants face when arriving and living in the United States, they continue to demonstrate great resolve to stay. They learn the language and customs, engage in the workforce, fight against discrimination, further their education, and champion others in an effort to live the American Dream. If you are an undocumented youth, keep moving forward. Stay positive, get the help you need, and never stop dreaming.

GLOSSARY

ally A person who unites with another and shows support.

asylum Protection granted by a government to a political refugee who is escaping prosecution.

citizenship The act of having all legal rights, privileges, and permission of a particular country.

defer The act of postponing something until a later time.

discrimination The act of treating someone differently than others without a legitimate reason.

exploitation The act of using or manipulating someone or something for one's own benefit.

immigrant A person who moves from one country to permanently settle in another.

liable To be held legally accountable or responsible.

migrate The act of moving from one country to another, either temporarily or permanently.

non-immigrant visa An official document that gives a qualifying foreign individual limited permission to travel to the country for a purpose, such as work, schooling, or vacation.

persecution The unfair and continual treatment of others by a government or uncontrollable group of people.

pro bono Performing legal work for free or a minimum charge.

racial profiling A form of discrimination that suspects a group of people of a crime or offense because of their race or cultural background.

refuge Protection from a distressful or dangerous situation.

repression The act of controlling someone or something with threatening force.

seizure A medical state of unconsciousness and uncontrolled body movements.

stipend A fixed amount of money that is regularly paid to an individual.

union A group of employees that is put together to protect the rights and interests of the members.

visa A government-issued document that outlines specific terms of your stay in a foreign country.

warrant A legal document that gives government officials permission to enter a home, perform a search, or make an arrest.

FOR MORE INFORMATION

American Psychological Association (APA)
750 First Street NE
Washington, DC 20002-4242
(800) 374-2721
Website: http://www.apa.org/

*Since 1892, the APA has been advancing the creation, commu-
nication, and application of psychological knowledge. It promotes
research, establishes ethics, and shares this information in public
forums and written publications.*

Canadian Citizenship & Immigration Resource Center
      (CCIRC), Inc.
4999 Ste-Catherine Street West, Suite 515
Montreal, QC H3Z 1T3
Canada
(514) 487-2011
Website: http://www.immigration.ca/en/

*The CCIRC website offers consultations on all things regarding
investing, living, studying, working, and settling in Canada.*

Canadian Immigrant
3145 Wolfedale Road
Mississauga, ON L5C 3A9
Canada
(905) 273-8111

8508 Ash Street
Vancouver, BC V6P 3S4
Canada

(604) 872-0102
Website: http://canadianimmigrant.ca/
This online and print resource to helps immigrants settle in Canada. It offers resources, tools, and strategies for personal growth and success.

Educators for Fair Consideration (E4FC)
c/o Community Initiatives
354 Pine Street, Suite 700
San Francisco, CA 94104
(415) 787-3432
Website: www.e4fc.org
E4FC helps undocumented young people pursue their dreams of college, career, and citizenship in the United States.

Mexican American Legal Defense and Education Fund (MALDEF)
634 S. Spring Street, 11th Floor
Los Angeles, CA 90014
(213) 629-2512
Website: http://www.maldef.org
This civil rights organization, which has fought for the rights of the Latino community since 1968, provides several scholarships for students who want to take up the cause.

National Association of Counsel for Children (NACC)
13123 E. 16th Avenue, B390
Aurora, CO 80045
(888) 828-NACC (6222)
Website: http://www.naccchildlaw.org
The NACC is a non-profit child advocacy and professional membership association that works to improve the lives of children and

families through high-quality legal representation and other forms of advocacy.

National Immigration Law Center (NILC)

P.O. Box 70067

Los Angeles, CA 90070

(213) 639-3900

Website: https://www.nilc.org

Since 1979, the NILC defends and advances the rights of low-income immigrants. Its services include trainings, publishing educational materials, and providing legal counsel and strategic advice to group-oriented advocacy work.

United We Dream

1900 L Street NW, Suite 900

Washington, DC 20036

Website: http://unitedwedream.org

United We Dream is an immigrant youth–led organization that consists of more than 100,000 immigrant youth and allies, as well as 55 affiliate organizations in 26 states.

US Citizenship and Immigration Services (USCIS)

995 Hardt Street

San Bernardino, CA 92408

(800) 375-5283

Website: http://www.uscis.gov

This government agency oversees lawful immigration to the United States.

WEBSITES

Because of the changing nature of internet links, Rosen Publishing has developed an online list of websites related to the subject of this book. This site is updated regularly. Please use this link to access this list:

http://www.rosenlinks.com/411/immi

FOR FURTHER READING

Bickerstaff, Linda. *Smart Strategies for Saving and Building Wealth*. New York, NY: Rosen Publishing Group, Inc., 2015.

Coan, Peter Morton. *Toward A Better Life: America's New Immigrants in Their Own Words From Ellis Island to the Present*. Amherst, NY: Prometheus Books, 2011.

Dreby, Joanna. *Everyday Illegal: When Policies Undermine Immigrant Families*. Oakland, CA: University of California Press, 2015.

Engle, Margarita. *Enchanted Air: Two Cultures, Two Wings: A Memoir*. New York, NY: Atheneum Books for Young Readers, 2015.

Gonzales, Roberto G. *Lives in Limbo: Undocumented and Coming of Age in America*. Oakland, CA: University of California Press, 2016.

Gottfried Hollander, Barbara. *Paying for College: Practical, Creative Strategies*. New York, NY: Rosen Publishing Group, Inc., 2010.

Hauser, Brooke. *The New Kids: Big Dreams and Brave Journeys at a High School for Immigrant Teens*. New York, NY: Free Press, 2012.

Kleyn, Tatyana. *Immigration: The Ultimate Teen Guide (It Happened to Me)*. Lanham, MD: Scarecrow Press, Inc., 2011.

Levy, Janey. *Illegal Immigration and Amnesty*. New York, NY: Rosen Publishing Group, Inc., 2010.

Manuel, Jose, Cesar Pineda, Anne Galisky, and Rebecca Shine, eds. *Papers: Stories by Undocumented Youth*. Portland, OR: Graham Street Productions, 2012.

McCormick, Lisa Wade. *Frequently Asked Questions About Growing Up as an Undocumented Immigrant (FAQ: Teen Life)*. New York, NY: Rosen Publishing Group, Inc., 2012.

Nicholls, Walter. *The DREAMers: How the Undocumented Youth Movement Transformed the Immigrant Rights Debate*. Palo Alto, CA: Stanford University Press, 2013.

Osborne, Linda Barrett. *This Land Is Our Land: A History of American Immigration*. New York, NY: Harry N. Abrams, 2016.

Padilla Peralta, Dan-el. *Undocumented: A Dominican Boy's Odyssey from a Homeless Shelter to the Ivy League*. New York, NY: Penguin Press, 2015.

Perez, William. *Americans by Heart: Undocumented Latino Students and the Promise of Higher Education*. New York, NY: Teachers College Press, 2012.

Porterfield, Jason. *Teen Stress and Anxiety*. New York, NY: Rosen Publishing Group, Inc., 2014.

Prentzas, G. *Smart Strategies for Paying for College*. New York, NY: Rosen Publishing Group, Inc., 2015.

Rank, Mark Robert, Thomas A. Hirschl, and Kirk A. Foster. *Chasing the American Dream: Understanding What Shapes Our Fortunes*. New York, NY: Oxford University Press, 2014.

Rennekamp, Rose. *Cut College Costs: How to Get Your Degree—Without Drowning in Debt*. North

Charleston, SC: CreateSpace Independent Publishing Platform, 2014.

Staley, Erin. *Defeating Stress and Anxiety*. New York, NY: Rosen Publishing Group, Inc., 2016.

Thorpe, Helen. *Just Like Us: The True Story of Four Mexican Girls Coming of Age in America*. New York, NY: Scribner, 2011.

Truax, Eileen. *Dreamers: An Immigrant Generation's Fight for Their American Dream*. Boston, MA: Beacon Press, 2015.

Zayas, Luis. *Forgotten Citizens: Deportation, Children, and the Making of American Exiles and Orphans*. New York, NY: Oxford University Press, 2015.

BIBLIOGRAPHY

American Psychological Association. "Undocumented Americans." YouTube video, 10:11. January 23, 2013. (https://www.youtube.com/watch?v=LFVoxezIxLU).

American Psychological Association, Presidential Task Force on Immigration. "Crossroads: The Psychology of Immigration in the New Century." *American Psychological Association*, 2012. Retrieved April 21, 2016. http://www.apa.org/topics/immigration/immigration-report.pdf.

APA Presidential Task Force on Immigration Members. "Working with Immigrant-Origin Clients: An Update for Mental Health Professionals." *American Psychological Association*, 2013. Retrieved April 12, 2016. http://www.apa.org/topics/immigration/immigration-report-professionals.pdf.

BestColleges.com. "College Guide for Undocumented Students." *Best Colleges*. Retrieved May 1, 2016. http://www.bestcolleges.com/resources/undocumented-students-guide.

Bray, Ilona. "How to Help a Detainee in an Immigration Hold." AllLaw.com. Retrieved April 23, 2016. http://www.alllaw.com/articles/nolo/us-immigration/how-help-detainee-hold.html.

Bray, Ilona. "Legal Rights of Undocumented Immigrants." Lawyers.com. Retrieved April 24, 2016. http://immigration.lawyers.com/general-immigration/legal-rights-of-illegal-immigrants.html.

Galvan, Christina. "What Happens When an Undocumented Immigrant Is Caught." Nolo.com Retrieved April 21, 2016. http://www.nolo.com/legal -encyclopedia/what-happens-when-undocumented- immigrant-is-caught.html.

Geraldino, Duarte. "Undocumented Entrepreneurs: No Social Security Number, Owning a Business." *Aljazeera America*, March 2014. Retrieved May 14, 2016. http:// america.aljazeera.com.

"Giving the Facts a Fighting Chance: Addressing Common Questions on Immigration." *American Immigration Council*, December 2015. Retrieved April 21, 2016. http://immigrationpolicy.org/special-reports/addressing -common-questions-on-immigration.

Hangartner, Morgan. "Green Card Through Cancellation of Removal (Non-LPR): Who Qualifies?" nolo.com. Retrieved August 25, 2016. http://www.nolo.com/ legal-encyclopedia/green-card-through-cancellation -removal-non-lpr-who-qualifies.html.

"Immigration: Finding Help, Giving Help." PBSKids .org. Retrieved April 24, 2016. http://pbskids.org/ itsmylife/family/immigration/article7.html.

Krogstad, Jens Manuel, and Jeffrey S. Passel. "5 Facts About Illegal Immigration in the US" Pew Research Center, November 2015. Retrieved April 21, 2016. http://www.pewresearch.org/fact-tank/2015/11/19/5 -facts-about-illegal-immigration-in-the-u-s.

"Legal Help: Help for Undocumented Immigrants." LoveIsRespect.org. Retrieved April 23, 2016. http://www.loveisrespect.org/legal-help/help-for-undocumented-immigrants.

"Life After College: A Guide for Undocumented Students." Educators for Fair Consideration. Retrieved April 30, 2016. http://e4fc.org/images/E4FC_LifeAfterCollegeGuide.pdf.

Pérez, Zenen Jaimes. "Removing Barriers to Higher Education for Undocumented Students." Center for American Progress, December 2014. Retrieved April 25, 2016. https://www.scribd.com/doc/246479454/Removing-Barriers-to-Higher-Education-for-Undocumented-Students.

Tamer, Mary. "The Education of Immigrant Children." Harvard Graduate School of Education, December 2014. Retrieved April 24, 2016. https://www.gse.harvard.edu/news/uk/14/12/education-immigrant-children.

"Top 10 Ways to Support Undocumented Students." *Educators for Fair Consideration.* Retrieved April 26, 2016 (http://www.e4fc.org/images/E4FC_EducatorTop10.pdf).

US Department of Justice. "1908. Unlawful Employment Of Aliens—Criminal Penalties." Offices of the United States Attorneys. Retrieved May 14, 2016. https://www.justice.gov/usam/criminal-resource-manual-1908-unlawful-employment-aliens-criminal-penalties.

Vargas Llosa, Alvaro. "Addressing and Discrediting 7 Major Myths About Immigration." Forbes, May 2013. Retrieved May 2, 2016. http://www.forbes.com/sites/realspin/2013/05/29/addressing-and-discrediting-

7-major-myths-about-immigration/#2f6672ae3810.

"What to Do If ICE Comes to Your Door?" United We Dream. Retrieved May 21, 2016. http://unitedwedream.org/blog/ice-comes-door.

"Why Don't They Just Get in Line?" American Immigration Council, March 2013. Retrieved May 29, 2016. http://www.immigrationpolicy.org/just-facts/why-don%E2%80%99t-they-just-get-line.

INDEX

ABOUT THE AUTHOR

After running a successful dance program for over a decade, Erin Staley took her stories from the stage to the page as a writer. Forever a student of the human condition, Staley fostered a passion for history, technology, and the enduring spirit of pioneers in their fields of interest. Today, she writes for the University of California, Riverside, as an International Recruitment Creative Copywriter.

PHOTO CREDITS